Lachlan Brown | Limited Cities

New Poems

GIRAMONDO POETS

Lachlan Brown | Limited Cities

First published 2012
from the Writing & Society Research Centre
at the University of Western Sydney
by the Giramondo Publishing Company
PO Box 752 Artarmon NSW 1570 Australia
www.giramondopublishing.com

Designed by Harry Williamson
Typeset by Andrew Davies
in 10/16.5 pt Baskerville

Printed and bound by SOS Print + Media
Distributed in Australia by NewSouth Books

National Library of Australia
Cataloguing-in-Publication data:

Brown, Lachlan 1981–

Limited Cities / Lachlan Brown

9781920882938 (pbk)

A821.3

For Corinne

In memory of Noel Rowe, who gently persuaded
me to open an account with poetry
SDG

Acknowledgements

Poems in this collection previously appeared in *Creation, Coolabah, HEAT, Hermes, Mascara, Philament, Relief, Snorkel, Southerly, Total Cardboard, Westside* and *5 Poetry Review. Evensong* was commissioned by The Red Room Company for its *Nightwriting* event and 'Epiphany' for its *Disappearing* app. My thanks to David Brooks and Ivor Indyk for their encouragement and advice, and also to the Westside young writers' group. Many of these poems were written in Barcelona and Paris with the aid of a Marten Travelling Bequest.

This project has been assisted by the Commonwealth Government through the Australia Council, its arts funding and advisory body.

Australian Government

Australia Council for the Arts

Contents

Onramp

Urban Sprawl

Macquarie Fields. Spring's edge 2004

Give me corrugated iron & grinning billboards
& a day as brilliant as a fire escape. It's been raining
for a week, but now the clear sky curves overhead
like a fruiterer's expansive arm. The ducks understand,
paddling in a creek flushed with prams & plastic &
spectating blackberries that sprawl on banks.
Train's delayed, but I'm feeling generous, as a
toddler laughs & snatches at the air – *when i used to*
get bigger i *had one* – it's the logic of the day, like
exams ending or the local paper spilling ads onto
the carriage seat. Outside the cameos glide past. Sunlight
& breeze & green lawns winking. Businessmen talk
of outsourcing,
but the windows snare their gaze, along with a pretty
girl wearing ripped jeans and a face like a pretty girl.
If you die then you can't go shopping. Not bad advice
when the timetable stretches like chewy under the seat or
a commuter's double yawn. There's that feeling, on the
edge of
your skin, as the train slides in smooth archaeology, gently
brushing lines overhead. Looking out from under
your sunnies you could be a bass player, laying down
an easy groove that squeezes around headphones
and tracks footprints through carriage minds.
Meanwhile each station's concrete sparkle greets

a morning flecked with toothpaste and cool breathing
and there should be a soundtrack to all this/ perhaps
the promise of empty pages and not just the train
braking with a sigh.

Macquarie Fields. Autumn's edge 2005

Creative as a cardboard Santa, or a battle-axe block. That's
enterprise the Australian Way. It's on the news though,
jostling Oscar-winners and royalty for the top spot. I'm
beginning to rue the classified style & links that fold back on
themselves. All around us communities are losing the art
of mowing. *Tragique*! And yet there are alternatives:
interior design at the local Chinese, or green electrical
boxes sprayed with tags and sets of dangling legs at
dusk. Don't tell me you're not a fan of fireworks, or
fence palings spiralling into an officer's
shield? Around the corner someone lights a
mattress and two million TVs flicker like post
office gossip. Next they're wheeling in the news vans,
but kids on bikes crowd out reporters whilst the
rest of us string together theories about
bulldozers and ghettos and why our church has
no chance of attracting a minister now. Tomorrow
it might be more like 'failed social experiment'
and scrounging for a tenner to blow at
the TAB. But until then helicopters circle

and drone like half hour headlines, or four Saturday morning Victas trying to outdo one another. The reality is at the end of the day it's Us and Them... except for the good ones. Meanwhile hooded kids throw rocks 'the size of large golf balls' as members of the gated community putt to save par on the other side of the tracks. I'm somewhere in between I think, like a fallacy. Wrestling with the distant cheers that accompany each firework, and watching the bricks sail silently off screen.

Burn

And the wind is hot, it is summer in
advance, tearing branches like a string
section opening Mahler's Sixth.
A bird draws its line across the hardening sky.
A bus passes its shadow over driveways and
unfinished gardens.
You agree that there will be flames:
the shards of a broken bottle directing
light to the heavens and the earth
and cigarette ash twitching in the grass.
There are days when civilisations will end.
The wood is dry and stacked alongside the city
and quiet mouths begin to devour edges.

Coming Home

That bloke looks like someone I know,
like a journal I should be writing. I'm
lucky though, caught in that historical
moment where bass solos actually sing.
Maybe it's time to join the inner city
crowd – but the skyline
gets me, drags me back. Gums spread
out over James Meehan, radiant in the
day's last gasp like jewellery in a pawn
shop window, or literature before it's
thrown through classroom doors. You've
still got metronomes out here, along with
an hour's train trip to smooth over
abstract thinking. Now sleep's approaching
next to a world drawn through newspaper
headlines. Outside the kikuyu snares through
silent garden beds and all of Sydney's given up
on causes. Time to settle for ulterior motives
then. Theorists lining up late like Thursday
night wheelie bins. And this chessboard suburb,
where every lung expands and contracts
with its own economy; each breath another
loan repayment, or a tax deduction
blinking like a cursor.

Love Song

Air, breathing. I walk
and it's not like Paris
where each car has
dimples from years
of close parking. O
my love! This day of
flawless duco and
Australian distances.
And all around, new
Life: birds sing, flowers
bloom and midriffs burst
from jeans like deployed
airbags. The sun
grins through winter's
back door, and the
sounds arrive like
invited guests at a party:

1) through headphones
a piccolo snare is
opening up the world.

2) a couple is having
a mathematical conver-
sation. '... a triangle of
tolerably equal sides'
...

'I like the way that
factorials always
look so excited!'

3) a stationwagon
sighs and lowers
itself into a gravel
driveway.

4) somewhere a
pageant contestant
describes herself as
'an RV girl with
a futuristic heart.'

5) a plane dips low
over the inner west,
just like a bad
neighbour screaming
'take that house
prices! take that!'

Sing, sing! As if the sky
were some giant plastic
microphone, just
waiting to receive your voice.

Meredith

Dark forces dragged you cliffwards collapsed the rock
you were resting on, sending you tumbling
into the unknown. It was unanimous, the screams
and splintered bones, shards of light
filtering down through the canopy,
bell-birds refusing to sing and the myth of
gravity, holding down lungs with a fat, flat palm.

Kerbside

Poem for a Film

1

Like a lo-res rainbow, stuck to the
screen of someone's mobile phone

I dreamt that my alarm had sounded
and that I had forgotten the code

my ears were ready too, for a high pitched
siren that never began, and anyway

on waking, a security pass had split,
its two halves sliding over one another

like yesterday or the day before when my car
almost spun out, somewhere in the backstreets

of Prestons where sleepy mansions crowd the
edges of blocks and artificial bends shape chicken-

farmed land with new and beautiful truths.
I think my tyres need changing, because I may

have lost my grip on all this, you know when
the world starts to spin? I'm seeing stars in

the sky and in those counterfeit newspapers
that flutter in carriages, heading out west.

2

Of course, you do admit that we are
retelling the same stories, for instance

the one about peak-hour traffic and
some dumb shit of a driver, cutting

across four lanes, eyes on a text message
thrown up by a shiny black phone,

and the edge of the road that is lined with
litter as though this were the aftermath

of some kind of parade, and so
now one silver hatchback trawls the

left hand lane, its eternal blinker
repeatedly pointing out the problem.

And if your hand were to become
a giant foam hand, then you too could

gesture toward all this important stuff,
an unheeded speedo, a crow searching

through fast food containers and
the trail of brake lights guiding you home.

3

To exist within this weatherboard valley
is to remain always six degrees from the

city. Here the kids pedal wide streets that
pretend to lead nowhere, whilst their elders

cultivate a nostalgia for sprinklers and
those ancient dreams that can never leave

this suburb. On a blistering afternoon
a council truck is removing tall trees,

so that no one will confuse this vista with
a place of moneyed elegance. And maybe

the scream of the chainsaw means you're
not ignored, as cut limbs crash through

the dry air. And maybe, what's left is
for your own good, and the streetscape

becomes a mouth smashed up during a bar fight,
with its bare stumps grinning cruelly in the heat.

Now each day you must arise in a dark place,
reminded by what we can do to greatness.

4

And after late night game shows
have flourished then disappeared we

are resigned to failure: those dubbed
movies, those advertisements for impotence,

those dating lines dribbling their phone numbers
into the morning. Outside drunk cries give

the blackness depth, shattering like bottles
hurled against a brick wall, and you recall

the sirens that ghost alongside your dreams.
Could it be that these are the only ways

to cash out a life? In a cell at the station
there is a bloke nursing a fractured eye

socket. He remembers nothing, except
glass & fluorescent tubes & a sign

saying 'Have You Seen Anything?'
Elsewhere, good people are finding sleep,

counting every interest rate rise and
rows of wooden letterboxes snapping shut.

5

Noon. The day has flatlined. The eucalypts
point their leaves toward hard ground, the

cars stop flying down the hill from Glenfield.
The shopping trolleys no longer clash

in the Coles carpark. And even the
truanting kids have stopped hurling

rocks onto carport roofs. You see,
they're all waiting for a breeze to jumpstart

the afternoon. But the day's like a Falcon,
chocked up in a front yard, it's like a gate

that's been welded shut because you know
we're not in Vaucluse or near some beach

where they film iconic Australian TV. You
know that within these cul-de-sacs you

have to earn any hint or breath of change. You
have to pay with sweat, with grease on

a two-stroke, with teeth set like wire cutters,
ready to meet the fenced-edge of the landscape.

Sonnet

Who starts a question with 'Question'?
But talking through the ad breaks is hard,
like remembering turntables when you're
not cool enough to be a DJ, or holding
style like a camera. I'm not worried
though, I've seen people so beautiful
they should be on reality TV. Lights
out, not flickering over the harbour
anymore, like ash dropped into black water
floating down from the side of a ferry.
But we're still yelling, and gunning it at
the lights as credits roll like mag wheels in
Bankstown. Maybe I'm wrong & we've peaked too soon
as rich kids laugh throw shame at the moon.

Petrol Stations, or Nine Vouchers Without the Optimism

It is as if a novelist of our day were to sketch a satirical
caricature of, say, service stations, treating them in
a ludicrous way.
Borges, 'Partial Enchantments of the *Quixote*'

1
No one knows
the entrance
or exit. So cars
          end up
nose to nose
like awkward
lovers:
double take,
reverse,
in gear, out
of gear.

Every time the
light turns
another one
swings into this
confusion
where affection
is measured

by momentary
politeness,
the crunching
of a car door.

2
This is the world
walled
by sheer glass,
by counter &
closed circuit cameras.

I am thinking
of the attendant's
dreams, but it's
not dreams
exactly
that offers a
space inside,
where margins
are higher.

3
Kids are brazen,
nonchalant,
pretending to
pretend to
skate in the

supermarket
car park.
Across the
road the servo
becomes
a temple
to sugar
& ice.
What is more
reassuring,
than the
snap & clink
of a car's badge?

4

No order,
created by placing
chocolates in
meticulous rows,
can withstand
the drifting
fumes
that ghost
through
the automatic
glass
door.

5
The thoughts
of passengers
left inside
vehicles,
with cares
that can't
be scraped
off windshields.

To hiss
like compressed
air
is to
invoke
the spirit.
Or is it
just
the day
rushing its
edges and
escaping
again?

6
The fullness
of all things is
8888.8888.

It might exist
in the moment
before the trigger
is pulled
and before
commerce
commences.
Is this
anything
more than
a hymn
to the event
that enacts
all possibilities?

7

The world's great
logos
often gather,
assemble in ranks,
service stations
begetting other
service stations
or acquiring
fast food outlets
as appendages
in the expanding empire
of Oil and Burgers.

No banner
can flutter,
but each will
glint in the
midday sun.

8

On a cold morning
a car will lean
into the day,
dip back onto
the main road,
struggle toward
each new set of lights.
Freedom means
roundabouts!
Or tollways!
Or a hubcap
left on a
roadside,
spinning like a coin.

9

Granted the end
must begin somewhere,
with numbers edging
upwards,

with the
apocalyptic click
of the bowser.

and instead
a surveillance camera
is staring down reality,
the world cowering
into grey submission
beneath
its single
determined eye.

Kiss Kiss Kiss

Catch this day in 120 characters,
160 if you're feeling generous. People
and announcements have caught me off-
guard. What's more, that broken triad
isn't gospelling any message of hope –
just that the economic station attendant
is the immanent station attendant. And
all of a sudden it's easy to imagine the
onboard intercom crackling with uncertainty,
and dozens of people running to catch the
bus I'm running to catch. Until then though,
it's immaterial, as tricky consciousness
peels images away from experience; those
kids skidding chips onto the tracks, that
couple drinking each other over a lone
suitcase, the gleam of a coin, scratching
persistently at the surface of the future
and the air
stirring, breathing with the last warmth
of summer, kissing skin like a cloud of moths
in transit, or thousands of tiny text messages
flying through the ether.

Afternoon

No shame past Sydenham, where
the train gets enthusiastic about small
corners. There might not be a fingerprint
of this day but someone's
probably trademarked 'this moment'
and 'thismoment.com' and
'thismomentmovie.com'.
Two tyres against a wire
fence would be holding hands
if tyres had hands. That's love,
not satellite dish and colorbond love,
but a heart mortgaged to the hilt.
Still the train's embracing every
swerve. Heads asleep, tapping
windows in the quiet morse code
of undeciphered
dreams.
Now Revesby (and beyond)
and this rhythm
        stacks up
and some kid's
        tagging the future
and all high school conversations
        are staged high school conversations
and the Glenfield dentist has
        a trembling hand-painted sign

causing someone to remark
that if the Glenfield dentist
painted that thing then you
wouldn't really want the
Glenfield dentist holding a
drill near your teeth
and train doors open onto
solid platforms repeatedly
and from somewhere the clouds
appear and smear themselves
across the afternoon sky.

Replacement

Almost a Dream

I am carried by a crowd into a square,
and they are speaking a language that
is not my own. Their flags and banners
wave with anger and resolve, and a
microphone discovers someone's
new voice. Hands are waving. We are
pressed close to others. Policemen with
handguns and worried eyes attempt to
move people on. All around us white
buildings are lit by hidden sources, as
if governing could be this secure and calm.
I want to believe so much, but I look up
and see the moon. It is full and passed by
small clouds and made for nights like this.

Lullaby

And at last I have found an evening,
where the train becomes a string of lit
beads, drawn across tracks by an unseen
hand. To return with a suitcase, and the
murmurs of the carriage is to arrive
alongside companions who are always to
hand. In a seat behind me, reunited lovers
are discovering an uneasy silence,
realising that the night is no longer the same,
that the winter hides the moon beneath its
coarse cloak. A palm is placed upon the
glass, and the window speaks its warning.
There is a chill that threatens to pour into
all of life: your limbs, this carriage, the
tracks of steel that disappear behind us.
And all of us know the evening is vast.
It stretches into the distance, claiming every
space that exists outside whispered words.
And now I must sink lower in my seat, and
draw the sleeping world about my ears.

Disbelief

Listen, you sceptics! Take heed before you
crush the world with the cruel hammer of reason!
There is a young child in Paris who has
remembered the city streets by heart.
Every evening he recites them in his father's sushi-bar,
holding only a small directory that is seldomed opened.
Like a warlord he sends waves of delivery boys
onto narrow laneways, taking routes that
many have since declared to be impossible.
I have seen this child, kneeling upon a chair,
his small hands arranging a table, his lips
mumuring directions that must be followed.
He sits amidst steaming bowls of white rice, whilst
his father's quick knife slices through night and air.

Numbering the Days

1. In a park outside the city

Catch the loop around the lake
the ducks gliding in
considered pairs. We too are moving slowly
noting the daffodils
emerging onto the grass
like splashes of new sunlight
and the line of wooden boats
tapping out emptiness in one another.
What is our sky
with colours only half-remembered
with trees spindling the horizon,
mending its frayed edges?

2. Unhelped by any wind

I am not yet asleep
on this asymmetric night

and instead remain at the table
slipping on words beside an empty cup

Already I miss the gas hissing on the stove
and so I lean
an elbow against the wood
next to an unopened book

imagining its pages turning in the darkness

3. Could we sit all day?

The apartments know we cannot afford to be here

but they hold their peace
like gentle benefactors in linen coats.

Children pass on scooters
herding their grandparents
along each curved path
and the trees are now budding

in the slow prelude to summer
each recalling an ancient song.

4. Keeping it all going

O runners it seems you are helping the world in its revolution

your muscled legs
pushing against gravel and pavements

majestically overcoming gravity
with the seriousness of each step

Indeed you are no longer infants balancing on low ledges

limbs like dice
scattering with every fall

And, for moments, you leave those places which capture us.

5. On line two

Some things are clear
like when the carriage
bursts into graffiti and discounted sunlight

or a woman rises to leave
and her seat snaps shut
like a sharp rebuke or a director calling cut.

But later the breeze will catch the scraps of rubbish

so that they twist in the air
like perfumed unruly thoughts

6. Trying to recall the future

The snicker of a pigeon
taking off
pre-empting the moment of our departure.

Do you remember the sky above the buildings,
crossed
with the white trails of jets?

Who can interpret this cuneiform script
those small cuts in the fabric of the world?

7. When the planes are no longer flying

We are still here
                                      lying on the grass in Place des Vosges
where the rooftops frame
                                                     an empty blue canvas

where women flick cigarette ash
                                                             onto the ground
(perhaps unaware that this is just another waiting room).

See the leaves of the trees? Their green is trembling
with all these conversations that stir the air.

Some Things That Occurred Today

1. fish came close to the shore in schools
following bread thrown by eager children.

2. a hand traced a stone wall and the holes
carved by the ammunition of a remembered war.

3. we rose beneath a pointing statue to view
the city as it spread itself from dark hills.

4. some people on the television agreed
with one another.

5. the air-conditioner was switched off and
then breathed deeply like a smoker in a doorway.

6. waves found a dirty beach, breaking
until they called the evening over the city.

7. I discovered streets that turned back on
themselves, and so walked them instead of sleeping.

Five Stories

1. a woman was irritated on the crowded metro.
but she did not fully express her emotions.

2. workmen placed a scaffold over a laneway,
so that metal rested alongside brown stone.
I walked beneath and imagined the world collapsing.

3. there was a child who had grown too large
for his pram. he wept into his father's chest.
perhaps he was spoilt. perhaps he had lost something
he could not ever recover.

4. a famous man visited a hospital. a group of
journalists and photographers followed him,
claiming his steps with their black cameras.
he walked and smiled and joked. his wisp of
white hair shone in the afternoon sun.
this man was not famous to me.

5. we climbed a hill on the edge of the city.
rooftops tumbled into one another. the ocean
made the distance seem very calm. turning,
we discovered that we were not on the edge
of the city.

Italian Sonnet

'We have no crazy cow in Italy'. But
they did have Berlusconi & people
who supported the formula one like it was the
Catholic church. What can you do with cathedrals
that push their way out of the ground like
stalagmites in Milan? And breathing here is all wine
& bottled water (a frizzante scherzo perhaps?)
But the only Italian I really know is the
stuff they invented music with, so I'm back
sitting in the Conservatorium's cool underground
where Verdi echoes & soars out over the
Botanical gardens, pouring itself into the harbour
like Alexander's water on the desert sand or that
homeless guy's liquid lunch.

Today

a bus snatches the air
from in front of you
and a woman gasps
as someone jags across
traffic like a grinning
spark leaping the gap
between plug and socket.
unlike the street the day
is clear and up there
new glass buildings
cooly reflect sandstone
and sky and the white
trail of a jet signing
the heavens with a single
stroke. you wish you had
this kind of style, the
nerve to cut across lanes
or to stand with an
architect's poise. but
instead you're waiting for
the lights to change you
into something new.

Here Say

Another Year

Summer is here, in
the sheets of the *Herald*
squeezed between poor copy and
ads for the government. These days it's
ink stains melting bitumen & crumpled business
sections, echoing an 80s classic that has somehow
heaved itself into another year, sweating
on 120 bpm like a fat jogger/ all bulges and baseline.
Help, help! I really want this
night to laugh forever, or at least
to crack a smile, like a bottle
opening before dinner, or a dress that's
back in style.
But until then it's reruns, run-outs and styrofoam
containers, as the radio jumps & froths,
spilling beer-brained tunes out of car windows
on George Street. Here's some good news, though-

i) – fuel prices
should
drop
after the invasion

&

ii) – if you keep driving then you
don't have to pay for parking.

So save your money Rusty! Nocturnes
don't come cheap, and the North Shore
keeps peering at the Opera House &
willing it to swap places with the zoo.
What's more, one day we'll take off for some
suburb that's not on the train map
& we'll laugh hard and scoff down four
bucks worth of hot chips
wrapped in shadows & greasy
reviews of Tetsuya's.

darling.city.friday.harbour

Go walk the concrete shoreline where
cast brolgas gasp in their metallic
permanence, where a fountain announces
the weekend to itself, where glasses chink
and flash like cameras, setting off love's
atomic collisions and a thousand minor
boating accidents. You've been citied,
but you realise this too late, finding yourself
engulfed by a crowd in a narrow street,
now ducking into a hong kong DVD store
& hoping for a moment of relief. But here!
recreations of immense television events
appear on shelves, wrapped in ranks
of stammering plastic.
What region is this? What language
invents our own stories and feeds them
back down frantic spirals of piracy?
And all around you, in the reality
of actual life, underground carparks
snarl and loop, traffic catches
at mistimed lights, and girls tower
over the pavement in heels, grazing on
cigarette smoke and exhaust fumes.
Then a pub crowd surges and
almost spills the guts of the world,
which is that dumb permutations

engineer most details, like pokies
& genetics & search engines &
personalised plates on a fleet of
nissan skylines. And even back at
the harbour the water's a bitumen black,
dreaming of a massive skatepark and
a dozen youtube stacks.
(I can offer you nothing more than these endless
vistas, and the glory of their sonic lies).

Twenty Sestets

1.

This industrial area is like Wetherill Park industrial area,
a nowhere or somewhere with wide streets
and trucks reversing.

The Subaru centre, blessing its rows of Imprezas,
or the furniture wholesaler
where a flat-packed future will be
the brittle souvenir of wasted days;

who says our dreams can stretch out like a roller door
before it curls upwards and disappears into its automated self?

2.

She loves the commute:
the train noting down each suburb
in its book of air and patient doors closing over moments
of concrete departure.
A kid is spinning a pen around his fingers
and the universe is here
intent in its orbit, all eyes on
the whirr of plastic. She tries to remain still, to focus,
but it won't stop rocking,
the carriage, this world.

3.

A back door slams the night on its back

A dog barks stupidly

and manages to scatters its paws across a concrete passage.
Cars slow at a roundabout,

as though wary of those forces of

dispersion.

And behold! we exist chromatically,

like a mailing list

or hundreds of digital channels

throwing their light across darkened rooms.

4.

Here on the main street, two old men are smoking
and they release the ghosts of dragons

with each breath.

And it seems that the morning is recalling a colder
conversation,
casting itself back

to those words that somehow push against
the limits of ice and air. But now school kids arrive and

drift toward the station,

unfolding sleep from their limbs.

5.

The lawnmowers are calling from suburb to suburb
and fences click in the heat,
                                                  as though the sun
were a meter, slowly ticking
                                        through the earth's final minutes.

He stops and considers all this,
                                              the grass-stained afternoon,
the air thick as engine oil,

a complaint of dirtbikes skidding across the reserve.

6.

The traffic dribbles us home and it's like spittle running
down the chin of a coma patient
                                              whose head injuries flare
against the pressure gauge.
                                        Now the beds are full
in intensive care
                              and a minivan noses in from
the breakdown lane
                                  and we're scanning the radio's
unused frequencies, desperate for a channel.

7.

Evening in the carpark, the sky slowly matching
the colour of the asphalt,
                                        those empty spaces
still marked by white lines or clusters of trolleys
grazing the gravel surfaces.
                                                This world where
cockatoos riot in distant trees
                                            and then take off,
filling the heavens like the stars we do not see.

8.

His heart's beating
                        like a generator behind a temporary stage
and her hand is close to his hand.
                                                She flicks her hair and smiles.
Her friends are screaming and slapping the guys
wheeling off (not far)
                        and returning like night gulls.
Someone kicks an empty goon bag across the carpark and
he knows he's gotta go for it
                        before the fireworks launch his future.

9.

A kid kicks a footy
                    and his father is beginning to face facts,
a cigarette hanging limply from his lips.

The kid concentrates and thinks *this time*
                                        but the afternoon
cannot conjure greatness,
                    not here
where bindis run their fingers across the oval
where the shadows of goalposts reach out like dreams.

10.

                    His voice like a fist breaking
through a gyprock wall,
and her face blurring
                    with makeup and tears.

Slowly the hallway tests its emptiness
and she remains
                    holding the halves of a broken plate.

Outside a garbage truck is passing,
                                        setting down its bins

like a triumph of empty glasses.

11.

Rising early he
clears his throat in the shower
as though the new day could be shocked
into appearing
from within this glass, the steam
a veil between his returning self
and
the darkened house
its appliances on standby
its hours already mortgaged and alone.

12.

Come young warrior
can you stretch this constellation
across the tinted rear windscreen of a Daihatsu
Charade? Can you feel the weight of

those stars

carving their burden into your shoulders?
For no one sings of pale restitution
when there is
zinc layered over sunburn and hot sand underfoot.

13.

The pledge of a vending machine
humming like summer
                                        but now she is reminded
of an airconditioner shuddering and powering down
expelling the last of the office air
                                        and soon a truck
will brake hard on a toll toad
                                        where the traffic treads water
where the sun is a dipping coin falling out of circulation.

14.

In his dreams the cannabis plants
                                        are growing
uncontrollably,
                            snaking through keyholes & gaps beneath
doorways
              and sometimes this half-remembered fear arrives

at daybreak like a tight collar or a narrow street
where an L-plater picks out
                            a three point turn
as though training for caution in an empty universe.

15.

Her lovesong is a six-lane highway
the strings of a guitar or
the callisthenics of a cherry picker
as it reaches up
to tune the power lines.
Her lovesong is
a noisy minah
spamming an endless afternoon.

Her lovesong is the thin edge of this platform
where each train forges a new & timetabled reality.

16.

After the shower
the drainpipes are sobbing gently

whilst distant soldiers shoot blanks into
the Holsworthy scrub

and in his flight from memory
each longneck is a brown river
narrowing like a sniper's eyes
beneath the grey tent of sky
that loops over the railway

scoping out this yard
and its weeping rows of unopened bottles.

17.

She ain't misunderestimating
                                                  the romantic fanfare
of her journey home
                                    and those earnest attempts to
divine the future from every oil-stained carport.
O beautiful neighbour, he has edged his lawn for you!
He has trained his jasmine to wander
                                                            up trellises
casting shadows onto the stencilled driveway of your heart.

18.

Democracy's fictitious imprint means a campaign

poster still clings to its telegraph pole even after

the election has been decided and last night someone

walked down this street smashing every single car

window as though they were enacting a compre-

hensive victory or numbering boxes below the line.

19.

Late closing means he is in the alleyway

propped up against the fence
the sky a strip of electrical tape

its moon a dirty nail
Soon the dawn will crack

the night like a empty bottle
sending shards of light this way

and somewhere a subwoofer is shaking
with anticipation

his hands now trembling in their search for keys

20.

Those silent limits of grace
like the emergency phones
she passes on the motorway
like the soft landing of
the exit as she takes the corner in a wide arc
like those factories
with their gardens lit for no-one
and their soap-smells scenting the night air

leading her back to sleep's cool corridors.

Epiphany

tracking in a studio on the
northern beaches you know
that guerilla tactics have to
start here before the drummer
buries the click before you
begin layering vocals like
those cars backed up across
the spit bridge because even
now some things still offer
glimpses of prosperity for
example the water viewing
itself through the lens of a
developer or yachts nudging
one another with the wind's
optimism much later kids will
kick a gatorade bottle along the
platform at glenfield station
and you will wonder whether
it's worth concentrating on how
to play pocket because when
you are there caught between
the ocean and the cul-de-sac the
levels are peaking and you are
gripping irony's hard wheel and
somebody keeps asking whether
this is the jesus talk or the money

talk you know of course that you
should respond with *your best life*
pitch-perfect on a churning sea.

Recessional

Prosperity Gospel

In traffic
someone is let into a queue
with a polite nod of the head and the
day sideswipes grace near this part
of the city that is not
the city.

Yesterday
a truck burst into flames
on the F3, self-immolating like
a zealot or a garbage bin on a bored
summer night.

All of this
speaks to the world
of the human heart. And yet
I am reminded that it's getting
harder and harder to diagnose
these things.

For instance,
perhaps roundabouts are
breaking out all over Sydney
in response to a
higher call.

Or maybe
graffiti artists have turned
professional, tagging each
colorbond panel with meticulous
precision, like cells in
a spreadsheet.

But now,
as the city pokes its head
over the mangroves, people
are armed with the logic of
poker machines.

They are
exegeting the sketchy car
always parked at Seddon park,
or the wind catching a mullet at
East Hills station.

(and it almost works/ it all most works)

So this
week is meccano week,
and the days click together,
their moods stacking like
shipping containers.

And if
a real estate agent's flag flies high,
if a pensioner's roof has been restored,
can you even begin to question
why this city is
so assured,

As though
it were temporary fencing or
a tenacious volunteer at an annual
community event?

Yet in
the rain we miss things: large thumb-drops
pressing each flower into soft earth,
a raised eyebrow like an interrupted cadence
and along each
train line,

Sydney sandstone
weeping, weeping.

6 Advent Poems

Advent I

you're walking streets with
no ipod which must mean
travel and when the city
of lights lights it's hectic
to be here or even just turn-
ing the corner right after the
flames have died as the
fire trucks are arriving late
and their sirens throw more rays
on every wall every wall every
wall street knows it's the season
for layoffs they become more
deadly near christmas and this
means share prices are falling
like snow onto dirty pavements
you find yourself packed into
a large cathedral alongside death
and tourists and so you contemplate
death by tourists as *lumen de*
lumine projects great art and
icons onto a screen that cannot
be the mind of God in an outer
suburb a burnt out apartment
becomes a gash of black against
a massive salvific block and as

you walk it flares again in mira-
culous afternoon light and you
feel the discounted groceries and
the hands of trees and the emptiness
of this day and each satellite dish
reaching out for you and you alone.

Advent2

you find a city that is gripped
by an epidemic of shoestores
and long avenues lined with
impossible trees they assume
their thin lines in winter's black
against the sky at least that's
what your photos are likely to
say and yet brown boots have
grown thigh-high and every
bus shelter proclaims an un-
dying love for anne hathaway
except for the one at la courneuve
that has shattered and beautiful
glass covers a path near the
tricouleur and a roundabout you
know the way that salt covers
a street in the snow well that's
the way this glass has fallen to
the ground it's funny that the
hotels on the rue de rivoli are

in a fierce christmas light battle
indeed one can begin to live with-
in these contradictions a bus ad-
vertising pollock must pass by
buildings of pure white stone
or in st severin where mary the
mother of God sits beneath a
spinning disco ball so much is
convincing in this cold that fills
vast distances don't you think?

Advent3

in a burger joint in clichy
sous bois where the day is
killing us with cold one web-
site says 'feels like minus
seven' and this is true like
the internet is always true
outside it's raining and the
wind is ripping the last few
leaves from december trees
two kids sit nearby under a
tv showing edith piaf and
charles dumont as they sing
'les chansons françaises' then
one of the kids starts to echo
mon Dieu in a high-pitched
voice and they laugh because

they know how much that
song means the presenter says
'une belle chanson, no?' and
I'm grinning into the plastic
table cloth next they offer de
noël blanc and through the
window a corsar is starting up
its exhaust breathes in white
wisps exposing the cruelty of
the air to all those in icy bus
shelters who stare into the dis-
tance awaiting an appearance.

Advent4

every kid on the bus becomes
a dj with a cellphone and a jacket
pocket because you need a song
that can make sense of all this I
mean the way that the avenue de
sévigné curves like the seine all
silent and grey or the distances
that leave a wasteland between
apartment towers those structures
so large that they seem to test
the dimensions of the sky itself
and then there are the trees cut
in severe lines as if to redefine the
terms 'proportionate response'

they line the footpaths these trees
like american marines with short
hair and brutal faces what does it
mean when a quad bike screams
the night into existence skidding
around a set of traffic lights or a
crow cries and rises from a nearby
branch somewhere a good man
reminds us that you must not give
up all hope for an audi may flash
past or a crane might lift a great
weight and begin to build more
apartments and there is still the
mcdonalds with doors of polished
glass its arches like strong arms
and those three flags slapping the
wind in triumph and defiance.

Advent 5

it's hard not to think
of economics in any
city centre but perhaps
this one is better than
most the buildings cap-
ped like wages in hard
hard times as though
history were pushing
back against the forces

that direct capital into
towers of glass and
steel I know that in
this climate things are
cold but on rue st-honoré
the curators of expensive
gifts stare out like lonely
kids in empty playrooms
so that you almost want
to go in and buy a rolex
out of pity I guess we all
need to be rescued them
you me those guys living
on the airvents who smile
and bum coins knowing
they arrived at this point
well before the rest of us
even realised where the
funbus was headed some-
where a group of hooded
kids are throwing a basket-
ball so quick it could be
made of burning ice but
they are in a place that is
neither real or profitable
and so the train continues
scrolling like a news ticker.

Advent6

did you dream that cry
in the night the heavy
crunch of brick on glass
your sleep now cracked
open and silence streaming
through narrow gaps
there are faces with eyes half-
closed against the cold and
afternoons where grey towers
shepherd whole areas some-
times you sense that your
own presence wrecks this
cityscape and yet you con-
tinue to walk and look and
walk and now everything is
sore and like some kind of
traitor you can be found
where the rich live and the
lines are long in the chocolate
stores where a woman rides a
pink vespa that you could
park anywhere and she does
driving back the christmas
queues perhaps it is strange
that the wealthy are all eating
bread and you see a loaf that
costs many many euros and

you are reminded that you
can only know of this realm
through glass far from here
in the nineteenth a blue light
bounces off an icy pavement
and yet no one follows its path.

Evensong

O to be back in the suburbs at dusk,
beneath the red streaks that sometimes
line the sky with spray tan enthusiasm.
This is the day worn thin,
marked by the wind's sudden realisations
(trees are a nation state, a beard is horizontal).
Don't you know that winter means
passing houses during the family meal,
each hallway bathed in a television's blue?
Don't you know that we must live in the shadows
of great financial institutions?
But this pinstriped night
where stars bleed into city lights,
where planes could be writing
the evening sky somehow,
here each constellation scaffolds the canopy,
allowing the universe to find its breath
in imperious and strange relations.

6 Lent Poems

Lent I

the men crowd the metro's
exits their collars pulled up
against the city of night
and we're trying to make out
a solo the licks percussive like
the rain slapping the pavement
when our backs are turned I
am told that it is depressing to
shop at low cost supermarkets
the vegetables droop and wither
on the shelves and the scanner
is a heart monitor on a dying man
so let's go outside where the wind
takes the lead and rattles the
window shutters and sometimes
it's like the périphérique itself
is shaking the entire city and
the flash of cars is a tightening
tourniquet you cannot sleep when
this occurs recalling the press of
people at midday on a narrow
market street the closed-in
headphones that can block out
almost everything except that
hiss that leaks like gas from

an exposed pipe and somehow
you know the workmen will
arrive with morning lifting
scaffolding past these errors
taking us closer to the perfect sky

Lent2

clouds are dark to the west
of Invalides as buses push
away from the kerb and the
sovereignty of traffic lights
stops a Mercedes causing
someone to glance up from
his GPS momentarily amazed
at the changed sky the time for
national debate has apparently
begun the tricolore is flapping
over Napolean's tomb and you
tell me we cannot hope to settle
this now there is far too much at
stake there are pigeons shitting
over Montfermeil and there are
rumours of discounting on the
Avenue Montaigne every crisis
has its origins in architecture or
immigration or both can you
imagine the stream of people
returning to les bosquets singing

liberty's song prompted by the
RER's tuning notes and the
platform now wiped clean like
a brand new beginning and so
this dream becomes the evening
when citizens are safely in their
positions soothed by love and
small purchases and the silent
water rising to fill the streets

Lent3

a practiced iconoclasm
for there can be no pictures
of the palais de l'élysée or of
the american embassy or
else the terrorists may win
so turn around and face
hermès instead noting the
pinnacle of all handbags
resplendent in the light
and remember your shutter
speed isn't fast enough to
capture this studded leather
or this glistening street the
guards now changing their
posts with anachronistic salutes
and rifles slung across shoulders
at the orthodox cathedral a

young woman is pressing her
forehead against the glass in
the flickering light willing
each saint to respond and the
choir's taped voices rise against
the dark wood of time so that
when you leave you sense you
may have missed something of
great importance like democracy's
tall gates swinging shut or a sales
assistant spraying that perfume
onto a card onto your wrist onto
the air of this delicate world

Lent4

at the jardin du luxembourg
footballs are kicked against
the great gates and gold
paint threatens to flake off
just like blossoming trees
or remembered snow so
perhaps across the city these
assaults are already occurring
that is someone is always
chalking the pavement at
gare saint-lazare or pasting
posters to the sides of metro
tunnels whilst the skateboards

must clatter over bastille's
trafficked freedom O take
me to calm estates where
silent graffiti haunts the
midday breeze where spring
rain cuts through the sun and
a rottweiler sleeps outside the
doors of the supermarket we
all dream of these unclaimed
spaces the tabula rasa of a
disused sportsground or a wide
street in a guttered postcode that
blank stare of bitumen which
almost ends here the building's
the precious white noise on the
edge of consciousness and the
fenceline catching paper like lies

Lent 5

there are new temptations
meaning that you might
crash like a house of credit
cards these floors of fashion
stacked higher than most
buildings and combined
with a weak local currency
this is almost all we need to
fail and the rain dampens

nothing here heck even the
beggars wear givenchy and
some don't even try instead
they just sit at tables outside
cafés smoking cigars and
discussing philosophy or the
way that the university has
moved to an unpopular suburb
across the city in a narrow
street someone chucks a mono
at the lights forgetting that he's
only riding a scooter and people
laugh with that hard humour born
of commuting from foreign countries
because it's comforting when
the rich lack judgement or when
this place momentarily becomes
no-one's home or the eyes of a
politician begin to stir with fear
his voice now flowing swiftly
like river suddenly narrowing

Lent6

these small steps beneath the
budding trees the sun glinting
off the metal frame of the centre
culturel and you almost believe
in resurrection as the cries of

workmen shatter like concrete
blocks and young couples arrive
clutching their well-ordered
folders containing all the promises
of real-estate and now you see
that former buildings are being
torn down to accompany this
unprecedented period of regener-
ation so a crane's giant skill-
tester arm rips chunks from
walls and throws them against
the pliant earth in front of this bill-
boards arise announcing each phase
in the partnership between industry
and government and even the bus
driver has caught the spirit of
generosity allowing the unticketed
to ride for free on this new day
when the land is being redeemed
with the joy of a lost discount
voucher now found yet one block
away a patrol van slides between
two buildings six policemen staring
from its windows like jaded tourists
passing another monument to freedom

Outstretched Arms

for Noel Rowe

maybe I'm getting used to it   the drive down the M5
black bitumen as smooth   as any beach
the search for parking   in Randwick   heels clicking
in hospital corridors   and my brother's
measured breath   intensive care is
quiet like a library   where machines and nurses
speak in lowered tones   as if death was sleeping nearby
not to be awakened   we're trying to talk to him
but it's hard to speak to stillness
the doctors keep saying   you must remember
his coma score   was very low
though young people often surprise us

my youngest brother   should be studying for the hsc
    according to my parents
instead he carts   his dreadlocks and skateboard
past hospital security   and tries to chat up
the pretty british nurses
I don't know how to comfort him when he starts crying
so we don't talk much   about the accident
or the operations   that aren't succeeding
instead we argue about the radio station   in the car
or we tell stupid stories   trying to capture moments
in nets of cynicism   and hard-eyed laughter

sometimes we offer each other alternatives
I'd rather fail the hsc I'd rather fail uni
than have a body prised from a snarl of metal
lying silently beside me perhaps we're each remembering
backyard games of cricket in fading suburban light
or the three of us on bikes weaving through
south coast scrub on our way back to campfire & breakfast
after one operation the shunts probe
my brother's brain to measure the pressure
the doctors tell us that we each have an ICP of three
or six when we've got a headache now visiting time
is consumed by shifting numbers that seem to be
always rising like sydney real estate or a bad economy
one day it goes up to forty six
and I can hardly stand

when my mother was a child all she wanted was a doll
instead of a school uniform from a culture
that understood mixed business more than Christmas
now she explores the hospital to pass the time
finding all the cafeterias
the Eastern Suburbs views that gaze out over her childhood
and the distant blue of Coogee one day she walks
into a glass wall thinking it's a door
that should automatically part she isn't hurt
just dazed and crying for hours in the afternoon
a man sits outside the hospital doors

sucking in smoke and weak sunlight a day later his brother
stops breathing he can't cope when they turn
the machine off so they have to call security
to pull him from the nurses sometimes I think
I'm not coping well either
giving shopkeepers the wrong money and showing up for classes
an hour early a lady on the bus stares
out into Centennial park what are we doing?
she asks of no-one or everyone
I want to reply but instead look down at my hands
rolling my bus ticket and unrolling it again

as days click past we're finding tragedy
in each waiting room face sharing stories
and cups of tea over month-old wedding photos
where my brother grins in forty degree heat
gripped by a suit & tie and the speech he had to give
after the accident they had to cut his shirt off
my cousin returned it along with his watch
she hadn't looked at because someone said
if his watch is okay then he'll be okay every few days
another family leaves after someone else drifts
out of the habit of living they each wish us luck
as though death were some blackjack game
and you have to know when to quit the table

my father's got a bad habit of leaving felt-tip pens
in his top pocket so that they burst in the wash
most of his old shirts look like he's been shot
in the breast he writes down the doctors' daily reports
in the same steady hand he uses to work through
maths problems & calculations for fluid mechanics
I don't read any of them though afraid of seeing
an equation that won't fall out in a QED or answer
to be honest I can't bring myself to read anything
at all at the moment without feeling the weight
of a more urgent story instead I try to line
my mind with half finished crosswords
& whispered prayers thrown skywards
longing for outstretched arms and words
that european theory declares meaningless

someone suggests we see a movie to pass the time
and to miss the easter traffic
in it drew barrymore has lost her memory
and repeats one day endlessly
it could be the model for the way
adam sandler makes films
but my mother sobs during all the jokes
imagining a different son waking up
eyes glazed like hospital windows I wonder if my brother
will remember Jesus and that to die is gain

at the moment though   I'd rather the fruitful labour part
back on the dairy where farmhands sweat and swear
when cows won't shift   remember the suburban baptism
in front of smiling school friends?   cool water lapping
before plunging & rising   in a backyard pool
(salt water not chlorine)   under a grey sky at dusk
but now he's just floating   on his back
on a hospital mattress   sustained by breath
not his own   a family friend is
the chaplain at the hospital   one day he asks if he can
pray with us   over my brother
and anoint him with oil   it runs down my brother's
forehead like tears that stiches can't cover
someone at uni says   easter's the season for miracles
but more than three days have passed   and we're all still afraid

leaving his room we go for a walk   along the Coogee headland
wind bending grass   like a reefed handbrake
and throwing spray   into our faces
what is the Holy Spirit?   a boy with a plastic bucket and spade
asks his father   on their way back to the car
my ears strain for the answer   but the wind snatches
it and sends it
flying
over the cliff face
the sea always reminds me of *La Mer*   an orchestra
of salt & movement   I imagine myself at my parents' house

playing Debussy again   on the family piano
        The Maid with the Flaxen Hair
it's afternoon   and mum's cooking dinner
in the next room   looking out the window
I can see my brother   through the backyard's fading light
knocking nails out of fence palings   whilst overhead
the jacaranda is blessing   the lawn with its flowers
each falling gently   like a final dying note

